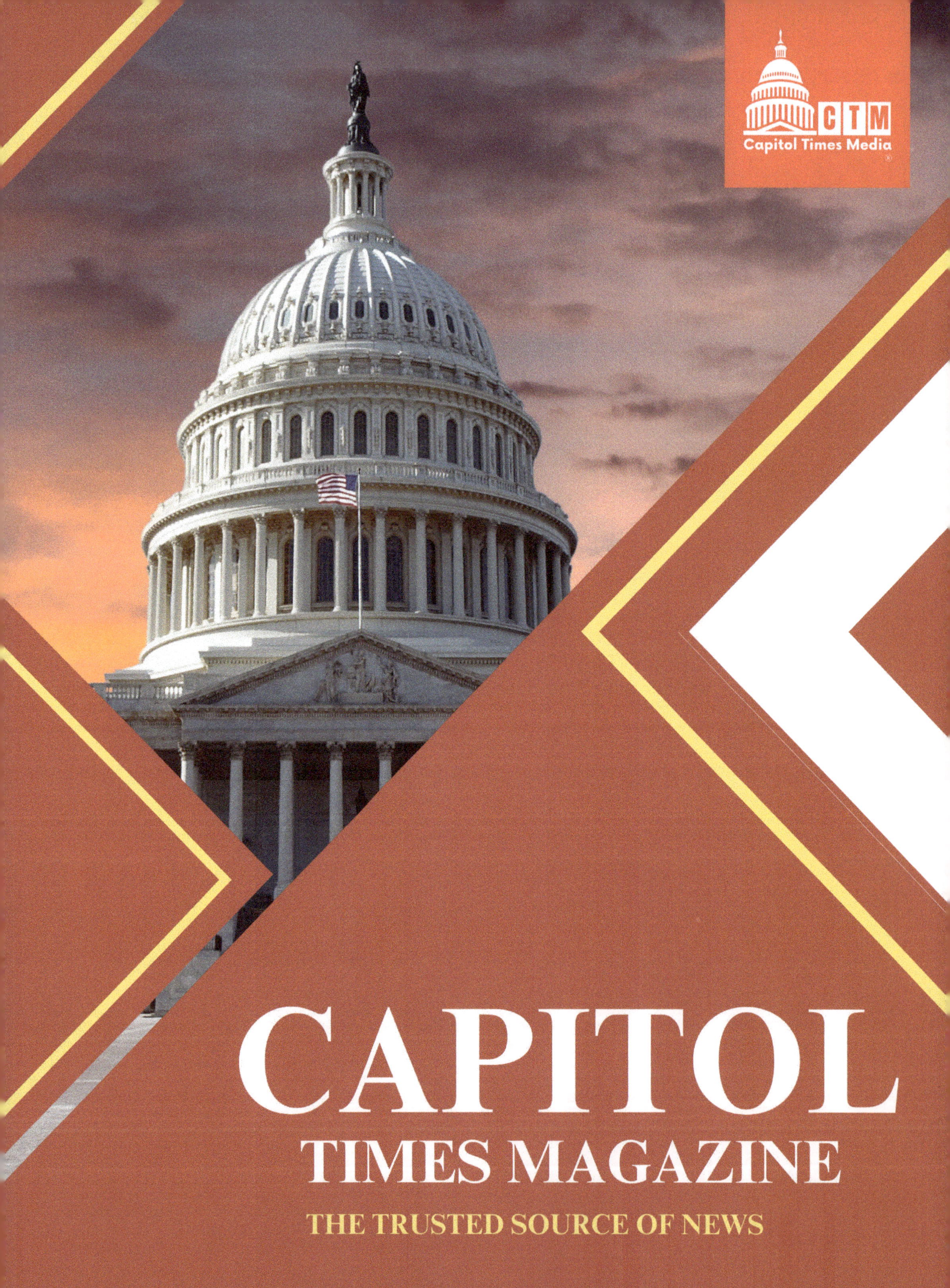

CTM
Capitol Times Media

CAPITOL
TIMES MAGAZINE
THE TRUSTED SOURCE OF NEWS

STAND WITH ISRAEL

SHOW YOUR SUPPORT FOR ISRAEL AND ITS PEOPLE

We believe that Israel has the right to defend itself against terrorism and threats to its security. Join us in supporting Israel's right to exist and thrive as a nation. Together for Israel

LET'S UNITE IN SOLIDARITY WITH ISRAEL AND ITS PEOPLE.

Let's extend our support, empathy, and prayers to the people of Israel, advocating for peace, understanding, and harmony in the region. Together, we can bridge divides and nurture a world where every individual, regardless of nationality or religion, can live in peace and security.

WELCOME TO

Capitol Times
Magazine

www.capitoltimesmedia.com

CTM

Editor-In-Chief
Anil Anwar

Publisher
Capitol Times Magazine

Magazine Graphic design
Sandra Clarke

Front Cover
Photo Source:
Christie Hutcherson

Image Attribution/Citations

Gage Skidmore
Wikipedia
Canva.com
The Israel Project
Pixbay

Capitol Times Magazine

Owned by Capitol Times Media LLC
Printed in the United States of America
©All Rights Reserved - 2023

www.capitoltimesmedia.com
editor@capitoltimesmedia.com

Review Rating

Thomas S

A must read. Turn off the TV. Sit down and read this. Then read it again.

Julie B

All Americans MUST read! This story is amazing and one every American must know.

Leslie D Keller

Important and great article on Patrick Byrne. Everybody needs to read this.

Review Rating

Martha Boneta

Excellent Magazine featuring Patrick Byrne.
Exceptional journalism and cover story featuring Patrick Byrne!

★ ★ ★ ★ ★

David Colbert

A Riveting Read: Capitol Times Magazine Unveils the Truth about the Deep State

★ ★ ★ ★ ★

It reveals shocking details about our intelligence agencies, our election system, and how our intelligence community seeks successful and powerful resources from the private sector to help them achieve objectives. America is in peril from foreign enemies and we must peacefully unite if we want to save our country. Time is running short for us to be successful.

★ ★ ★ ★ ★

Editor's Note

In this issue 3 of Capitol Times Magazine, we delve deep into the critical issues surrounding human trafficking, border and national security, featuring an insightful interview with Christie Hutcherson, a renowned expert in the field. As the world grapples with unprecedented challenges, it is essential to understand the complexities of border security and the imminent threats faced by nation today.

In our featured interview, Christie Hutcherson provides invaluable perspectives on border and national security, shedding light on the ever-evolving threats that America confront. Hutcherson's expertise offers readers a comprehensive understanding of the challenges posed by both traditional and emerging security threats, and the strategies essential to counter them effectively. Her insights are not only enlightening but also serve as a call to action, urging policymakers and citizens alike to prioritize the security of our nation.

In addition to our feature interview, this issue presents a series of thought-provoking articles that analyze US national politics from a conservative viewpoint. Our expert contributors dissect the current political landscape, exploring conservative perspectives on key policy issues, electoral trends, and the role of government. These analyses provide readers with a nuanced understanding of the conservative ideology and its implications for the nation's future.

In this edition of Capitol Times Magazine, we aim to foster informed discussions and encourage critical thinking about the pressing issues of our time. The diverse range of articles presented here provides readers with a holistic view of border and national security, US national politics from a conservative lens, and the global challenges that demand collective solutions.

We hope that the insights shared within these pages inspire readers to engage in constructive dialogues, advocate for informed policies, and contribute meaningfully to the ongoing discourse on matters of national and global importance.

Anil Anwar

Editor-in-Chief

more information: www.capitoltimesmedia.com

CAPITOL TIMES MAGAZINE

CONTENTS

03

OCTOBER ISSUE | 2023

www.capitoltimesmedia.com

NATIONAL SECURITY AND WITH OUR INTEL WE ARE EXPOSING THIS IMMINENT THREAT

Here is what Americans should know-

By Christie Hutcherson

editor@capitoltimesmeidia.com

www.capitoltimesmedia.com

Stay Informed with Capitol Times Magazine!

Your Ultimate Source for US National News, Right in the Heart of Capitol.
Grab Your Copy Today and Stay Ahead of the Times!

https://capitoltimesmedia.com

STAY TUNED TO OUR
Freedom
FOURUM
SHOW
EVERY THURSDAY - FRIDAY
8:00 PM - WWW.CAPITOLTIMESMEDIA.COM
FACEBOOK @CAPITOLTIMES | CTM NEWS
DAVID
COLBERT
Hosted by
REQUEST LINE:
972-591-8859
LIVE STREAM AT:
WWW.CAPITOLTIMESMEDIA.COM
FACEBOOK: @CAPITOLTIMES - (CTM NEWS)

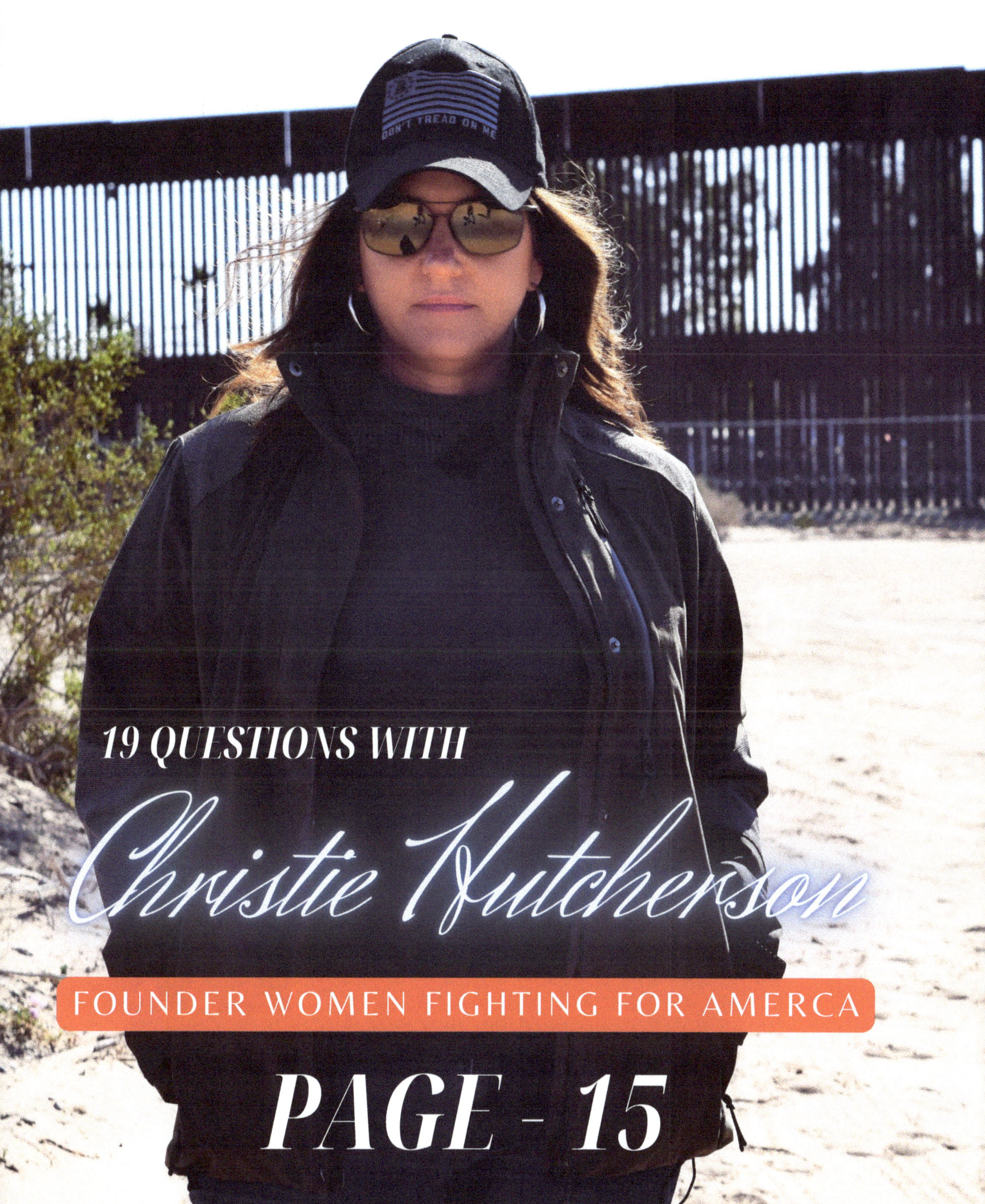
19 QUESTIONS WITH
Christie Hutcherson
FOUNDER WOMEN FIGHTING FOR AMERCA
PAGE - 15

"Christie Hutcherson is among the bravest and most courageous people I have ever met. She is fearless in her pursuit to expose the massive corruption and trafficking of human lives and illegal narcotics entering illegally through the U.S. southern border. She is a singular and fearless force to be reckoned with and daily makes a positive difference in the lives of millions of Americans. Without her expert skills and strong leadership, the United States of America would be even less safe and that says a lot."

- Michael Flynn, Lt. General USA (Retired)

"Christie is a strong patriot in the woman's movement motivated to preserve freedoms granted to us by our founding fathers. She realizes there is a war against our family unit; especially against the children of this nation. She works hard to expose corruption at the US border and corruption in the United States government. She is a shining example of the calling that women today hear as patriots and mothers to fight for what is right and God given."

- Patrick Byrne, Founder Overstock.com / Philanthropist

"To say Christie Hutcherson is a patriot is not describing the real woman in action. She's a fierce defender of human life, especially the people who are pawns of cartel operations profiting off the trafficking of women and children. Her focus on our borders has resulted in intelligence with national security implications. Christie shares that data with our US CBP and additional law enforcement agencies, resulting in practical and actionable counter intelligence resulting in the apprehension of drug mules, human traffickers and insight into cartel operations as well as threats to all Americans. I am proud to know this incredible woman, mother, freedom defender and friend."

- Ann Vandersteel, Co-Chair Zelenko Freedom Foundation

"Christie Hutcherson is among the most effective and courageous conservative advocates that I have had the pleasure to work with in my 40 years of experience. Christie and her organization Women Fighting for America have been in the forefront of virtually every vital public policy fight facing our nation today.

Christie has shown particular leadership on the issue of illegal immigration going so far as to put her own life and safety at risk in order to inform and educate the American people as to what is really going on on our southern border. I know of few selfless, brave and resourceful patriots who are as effective or committed as Christie Hutcherson. She merits both our support and our respect."

- Roger Stone, Political Consultant, Lobbyist and Author

www.wffa.win

CHRISTIE HUTCHERSON

Founder of Woman Fighting For America

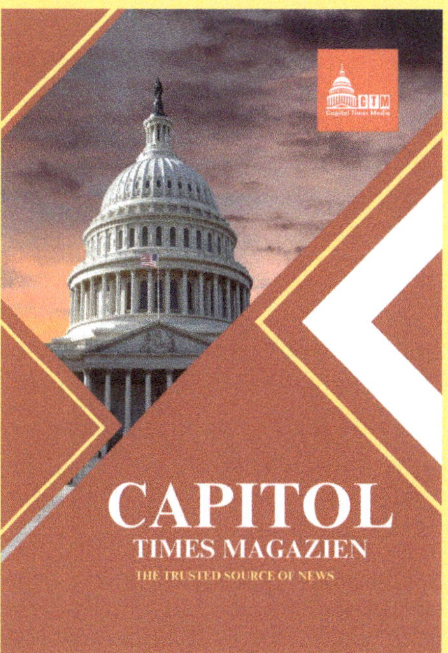

Ladies and gentlemen, welcome to Capitol Times Magazine. Today, we have the honor of sitting down with a remarkable woman whose courage and determination have made her a beacon of hope for millions across America. Christie Hutcherson, the Founder, President, and Spokesperson for Women Fighting for America LLC (WFFA), joins us for an insightful conversation. Christie is not just a name; she's a front-line fighter for freedom, a woman who has traversed the entire 2,000 miles of the southern border and countless miles along the forgotten northern border. Her experiences have given her a unique perspective on the challenges facing our nation.

As a geopolitical security expert and a sought-after speaker, Christie has led over 100 border missions, exposing the harsh realities of illegal immigration, human trafficking, and the infiltration of lethal drugs. Through her organization, Women Fighting for America, Christie stands as a staunch advocate for truth, promoting the Judeo-Christian foundations of government, educating without bias, and safeguarding the constitution. Christie's passion goes beyond politics; it's deeply rooted in her faith and her role as a mother. Driven by her Christian beliefs, she shines a light in the darkness, fighting for the future of our children, the protection of families, and the preservation of American values. Today, we delve into her journey, her convictions, and her vision for a united America. Join us as we explore the profound impact of Christie Hutcherson's work and the inspiring path she paves for women and the nation alike.

Photo By: WFFA - Christie Hutcherson

ANIL: What inspired you to establish "Women Fighting for America" in 2020, and how has the organization's mission evolved since its inception?

HUTCHERSON: As a Christian, witnessing the degeneration of our nation's core foundations was and is disheartening and troubling; the growing infiltration of Communist, Marxist ideology and continual suppression of freedoms and liberties stirred a rising conviction. Emboldened by my faith in the Lord, I chose to leave my former life as CEO of my company and step out into the mission field to serve. Women Fighting for America was birthed to promote the truth about the Judeo-Christian foundations of government in America, to educate without bias, to protect the constitution, and provide a platform to spread that truth. We have a strong passion to be a bold advocate for America, its soul, and its moral compass. We are passionate about the key role that women hold historically, which is currently shaping our nation's future. As a professional woman, our team desires to advance women's contributions and voices as it pertains to the American dream and culture. My role as a mother fuels my fight for education, the future of the children, the protection of the family, and the value it holds for American society. Our desire is to link arms with like-hearted women and others, establishing a collaborative effort. WFFA's moral compass remains steadfast and unshifting, our network, our relationships, our knowledge have grown in strength and in size, as we have been investigating the borders, policies and witnessing first-hand the corruption within our own systems we have adapted our strategies to include operational planning, technologies, and other tools to assist us in exposing corruption both internally and externally.

ANIL: Encouraging bravery and unity among women is central to your organization's message. Can you provide some tangible examples of how "Women Fighting for America" empowers women at the grassroots level to be the strength of their families and communities?

HUTCHERSON: Women Fighting for America is an organization that encourages fearless bravery, patriotism, and strong unity among women. Through grassroots demonstrations of empowering stories and narratives, women are supported to make a real difference in their families and neighborhoods. WFFA leads by example through real-life examples of the impact of bravery, courage, and activism in the world we all live in. With an understanding that these inspiring stories empower women to fight for a better future for themselves and their communities, the organization is setting the stage for real-world success stories of women who make a real difference.

Photo By: WFFA - Christie Hutcherson

ANIL: Your extensive travels along both the southern and northern borders of the United States are commendable. Can you share some of the most eye-opening experiences or discoveries you've had during these journeys?

HUTCHERSON: For the last three years, our organization has traveled the length of both the southern and northern borders. Along the way, we have encountered horrendous atrocities, human rights violations, and sustained threats to our national security. Our team witnessed firsthand the systems put in place by the drug cartels to aid their sophisticated operations.

One example of their operations: Our teams exposed highly sophisticated tunnels that ran the length of four football fields running through a highly trafficked border zone. This tunnel had fortified walls, ceilings, fiber optics, electricity, air ventilation system. This specific tunnel is believed to be used for smuggling drugs, weapons, possible bioweapons, and other material. Another example: our teams exposed active training camps for cartel operations, exposed rape trees, organ harvesting operations in Mexico, and visited areas where illegal substances and high-profile security threat persons are smuggled over the border into the U.S.

Our teams continue to expose the growing threat of China, Iran and Russia's influence and stronghold in the Central, South America and Mexico regions. Our team has been active in rescuing children from trafficking at the border, exposing NGOs (non-governmental organizations) and the corruption associated with their activity. The most frightening of all is the active willful participation of our own Government to undermine the safety and sovereignty of our country through their willful and anti-American policies.

ANIL: More than 10,000 undocumented migrants a day were crossing into the U.S. under the Biden Administration. As a recognized geopolitical security expert, how do you see the future of border security in the U.S. and its implications for national security?

HUTCHERSON: This administration would like the American people to believe that closing our borders and illegal migration is a complex issue, it is not. Closed borders save the lives of both Americans and illegal migrants. Open borders allow transnational criminal organizations to become emboldened, thus increasing their wealth and presence around the world, putting the U.S. and her allies at great risk. Open border security in the United States has serious implications for our national security. Without closed and secure borders, the U.S. is vulnerable to dangerous criminal activity, including the threat of terrorist attacks on our soil, and an influx of undocumented (illegal) immigrants and illegal activities that will forever change the landscape of this great nation.

These policies have allowed unknown numbers of terrorists to enter the U.S., creating pockets throughout our communities, including rapists, murderers, gangs, and cartel members. We have emboldened and, more importantly, allowed our enemies like Iran, China, and Russia to fill the vacuum within Central, South America, and Mexico created by this administration. The threat is here, and the threat is now! Our borders can be closed in 24 hours; the political will is not there. Through extensive interviews with local law enforcement and border patrol agents, they have informed WFFA that the Biden Administration has instructed the different agencies to not report the correct number of encounters at the Mexican border and the forgotten northern border. As a result, it is impossible to calculate the true number of illegal migrants entering the United States on a daily basis - This gap in reporting of crossings has created a chaotic and complex situation, as the number of individuals now entering the United States is exponentially larger than they are reporting. The American people have the right to know the real numbers, we believe they are upwards of 10 million plus. This is a planned active invasion.

ANIL: Given the increasing global concern about border security and the sovereignty of nations, how does WFFA collaborate with national governments to ensure that your operations respect and reinforce a country's laws and boundaries while pursuing these multinational criminal organizations?

HUTCHERSON: (WFFA) When conducting field investigations, we collaborate with national governments to ensure that our operations respect a country's laws and boundaries while actively pursuing multinational criminal organizations (Cartels). We recognize the increasing global concern around border security and sovereignty of nations and take these matters extremely seriously. Our secure and confidential partnership with national governments fosters an open, collaborative environment to help ensure that our operations respect and reinforce a country's laws while exposing these dangerous criminal organizations.

ANIL: The Women Fighting for America highlights several critical issues such as child trafficking, human trafficking, and youth indoctrination, among others. How does "Women Fighting for America" prioritize and address these diverse challenges simultaneously?

HUTCHERSON: Women Fighting for America is a movement committed to standing up for human rights and combating critical issues such as child trafficking, human trafficking, and youth indoctrination.

Through outreach, advocacy, groundwork and education, this movement provides a platform to highlight the injustices impacting millions across the United States and globe. We use our platform to expose those who exploit others. WFFA aims to prioritize and address these challenges by bringing attention and awareness to the issues.

ANIL: How does WFFA collaborate with local operational ground support teams to ensure the efficient interception of human traffickers in different regions?

HUTCHERSON: Utilizing the latest technologies - intel, recon, forensics, cyber-intelligence, ground operations, and through strong relationships with trusted officials - we are able to transfer real-time data with maximum efficiency. Due to the confidential nature of our work, however, specifics cannot be shared.

ANIL: What are the key challenges in waking the world to the scale of child and human trafficking, and how does your strategy aim to overcome them?

HUTCHERSON: Trafficking is a global issue, and it is difficult to create solutions that fully address the complexity of the issue. Our strategy is focused on creating awareness of the issue and identifying interventions to help break down barriers and create a more unified global approach to tackle trafficking. Every state has multi-criminal organizations who deal in trafficking, it is in everyone's backyard! WFFA has partnered with the Human Trafficking Training Centre to provide anti-human trafficking courses to citizens.

ANIL: Recognizing the conservative principle of strong and decisive leadership, how does WFFA ensure that its strategies to "crush the head" of these organizations are effective in preventing the rise of new traffickers or organizations in the vacuum that might be created?

HUTCHERSON: WFFA recognizes the conservative principle of strong and decisive leadership to ensure their strategies to "crush the head" of criminal organizations are effective. These strategies focus on mitigating the power and influence of these organizations, flushing out ways in which these criminal organizations operate. Due to the nature of our tactics, we cannot divulge further information.

ANIL: Under the Trump administration, there was a significant focus on bolstering American manufacturing and technological innovation. How did this focus help companies and organizations like WFFA stay at the cutting edge of defense and security technologies?

HUTCHERSON: The Trump administration had a significant focus on bolstering American manufacturing and technological innovation. This translated to substantial benefits for organizations such as WFFA, as the focus enabled them to remain at the cutting edge of defence and security technologies.

ANIL: How do your strategic partnerships with former NSA and CIA operatives contribute to the overall effectiveness and credibility of WFFA's operations?

HUTCHERSON: WFFA is proud to work with different agencies, law enforcement, global governments and private sector partners. These relationships are key to our credibility and trustworthiness in conducting certain operations. One such private sector agency who leads our security operations is Kennedy International Logistics and Services. With strategic partnerships like K.I., it enables WFFA to broaden its expertise and effectively deliver intelligence with even greater accuracy and efficiency, allowing us to operate in an atmosphere of high reliability and security. These experienced individuals bring a host of skills and knowledge to our business operations, allowing WFFA to succeed more effectively and efficiently while staying within the scope of established security standards. Our strategic partnerships ensure our operations are secure, reliable, and credible, enabling us to make informed decisions rapidly and create higher levels of strength (safeguarding). WFFA is committed to collaboration and works hard to continuously benefit from the collective knowledge, expertise, and experience of its valued partners on a global scale.

ANIL: Beyond raising awareness, what actionable steps do you see as necessary for governments, organizations, and communities to take in the wake of the exposure brought about by the embedded teams?

HUTCHERSON: Addressing the illegal border crisis requires concrete actions. The first action requires the complete shutdown of our southern borders until we gain operational control once more and protect it from serious national security threats, the exploitation of human rights, and the presence of trans-criminal organizations (cartels). This will ensure that the United States has the strength and resources to prevent any further stress within our systems. The US nor the free western world can withstand the burden long term that this created migration crisis will have on our own society, it is unsustainable and will eventually collapse our systems. Therefore, governments, organizations, and communities must come together to develop policy solutions to address the root causes of illegal migration and provide safe and secure access to basic services within their own borders. Furthermore, the protection of vulnerable populations must be a top priority.

ANIL: How does WFFA's foundation in Christian principles guide and shape your strategies to combat human trafficking and protect American freedoms?

HUTCHERSON: WFFA strives to defend American freedoms with a foundation firmly planted in Christian principles. These principles guide and shape the strategies that WFFA uses to combat trafficking. By utilizing the values of compassion, justice, and mercy, WFFA ensures that the freedom of every individual is held in the highest regard. **"There is an unseen evil in this world it has no prejudice, nor does it see colour**, economic status, or gender. It is called human trafficking after being on the frontlines and witnessing these unspeakable acts you can ever be the same. **Our organization will not rest until we put an end to this evil." - Christie Hutcherson, Founder Women Fighting for America**

ANIL: Could you elaborate on what you mean by 'counter liberal indoctrination'? What specific aspects are you aiming to address with your platform?

HUTCHERSON: WFFA seeks to provide an alternative, pushing back against the current education system's overwhelming emphasis on liberalism. We aim to offer students and citizens information and resources that help them understand conservative ideas and values, and to develop their own critical outlook. We are committed to offering a balanced and impartial view of current societal, political, and economic issues. We invite users to engage in thought-provoking conversations about political and social issues and to broaden their perspectives on global affairs. We want to provide a space for people to challenge and engage with ideas regardless of political ideology.

ANIL: You've mentioned a goal to 'reshape the hearts and minds of those 40 and under.' What challenges have you identified in reaching this demographic and how does your strategy address these challenges?

HUTCHERSON: Our strategy focuses on engaging with youth directly, rather than simply advertising to them. We are implementing advisory boards, open forums, and interactive discussion groups as part of our strategy to create lasting, strong relationships and understanding among youth. Addressing the challenge of reshaping the hearts and minds of those 40 and under involves connecting with them on a personal level. Developing strategies that consider their cultural, mental, and emotional needs can create an environment of understanding, allowing us to communicate our message and create impactful connections. By creating a genuine relationship and fostering an engaging and respectful environment, we can establish an environment that encourages growth, understanding and progress.

ANIL: In your fight against enemies, how does WFFA prioritize and address the threats posed by foreign entities that challenge American interests and values, and how do you see your organization's role in the global landscape to safeguard America's legacy and future?

HUTCHERSON: WFFA strives to use every tool in our arsenal to fight enemies and protect American interests and values, prioritizes security from foreign entities that challenge the values and interests of the United States. WFFA takes a proactive approach to this, engaging in international dialogue, diplomacy, and other tools to protect American interests. We see our organization as a global leader on safeguarding the legacy and future of America. WFFA seeks to shape a global landscape that is more secure and more in line with American ideals. We work to safeguard America's shining legacy and build a brighter and safer future for the next generations.

ANIL: The increasing polarization of the abortion debate, how can Christian conservatives engage in productive dialogues that emphasize the value of life?

HUTCHERSON: As I am pro-life, I value all life! However, the abortion debate continues to be deeply divided; it can often appear to remain a contributing factor to the continued polarization of our society. While it can be easy to become entrenched in one's own beliefs, Christian conservatives must strive to engage in productive dialogue with their opponents. Finding common ground in the value of life is key, which can be accomplished by seeking positive solutions that mutually benefit both sides. Christian conservatives can seek to engage in productive dialogue emphasizing the sanctity and value of all life. Individuals can recognize and work towards reaching a solution that not only respects the value of life but also allows for individual rights and freedoms, including the unborn's rights.

There are so many alternatives to abortion, adoption is just one. We must also engage with our state and federal governments to cut the red tape on adoption and make it a simpler process and less expensive. Children are NEVER for sale or slaughter!

ANIL: Can you share more about "On the Frontlines with Christie Hutcherson" on Brighteon TV? What are its primary objectives, and how does it align with the broader mission of your platform?

HUTCHERSON: On the Frontlines with Christie Hutcherson seeks to provide unbiased investigative reporting and analysis on news and current events. The primary objective is to bring awareness to overlooked stories and unique perspectives in order to challenge prevailing narratives. We have hard-hitting interviews with leaders who are shaping our world. This provides a platform for voices not heard in mainstream media, and by closely aligning with the mission of BrighteonTV, it hopes to keep viewers informed, engaged, and inspired. On The Frontlines airs every Sunday from 1-2 pm Eastern and Tuesdays from 4-5 pm Eastern.

ANIL: We've covered a lot of ground today, but as we conclude, what would you like the public to know most about your organization's mission and the changes you hope to bring about?

HUTCHERSON: Women Fighting for America is a movement dedicated to educating about the different visions for America. We support and defend our liberty and freedom and a vision of America where everyone can pursue the American dream. Today, Americans' closely held beliefs and freedoms seem to be under constant attack from mainstream media, elitist academia, judicial activists, foreign aggressors, and sadly many times from our elected politicians. These attacks highlight the two extremely different ideologies fighting for our country's future. Will we stand by and let America become a socialist, Marxist, or communist nation and give our children up to this hopeless vision? WFFA was formed to push back on the daily attacks on the nuclear family and defend American values and the constitution. I have seen firsthand the devastation of illegal immigration, child and human trafficking, organ trafficking, massive amounts of lethal drugs entering the United States, and the atrocities committed by transnational criminal organizations.

For more information about our organization, volunteer, give/donate please contact us via our website WFFA.win or email us at fightback@wffa.win.

NATIONAL SECURITY AND WITH OUR INTEL WE ARE EXPOSING THIS IMMINENT THREAT

Here is what Americans should know-

By Christie Hutcherson

BIDEN AND OBAMA HAVE GIVEN OUR ENEMY IRAN BILLIONS OF OUR MONEY TO FUND THESE HORRIFIC TERRORIST ATTACKS!

Iran has a huge footprint, and a very cozy relationship with Madura, matter fact, Madera traveled to Iran in March. This footprint has been further increased in Central and South America for the last 12+ years. Including Bolivia where there are military operations and storage facilities. Bolivia's president Novillo recently got back from a trip from Tehran, where he signed a defense and security cooperation agreement. This set off alarms throughout the border countries of Bolivia.

He has become quite cozy with Mohammad Reza, Qatari Ashtiani, which is the defense minister of Iran. This agreement will supply Bolivia with lithium, missiles, weapons, UAVs and intelligence in cyberspace. Among other things.

Iran has also been providing Venezuela with Iranian precision-guided missiles fitted into "advanced Iranian Mohajer" drones.

(Iran has a history of providing ongoing support to certain countries in Central and South America. For instance, in 2008, Turkish officials seized 22 containers bound for Venezuela, which

were labeled as tractor parts, but in the container were materials for explosive laboratories. Additionally, last summer, one of the US sanctioned airlines were supposedly carrying auto parts, instead highly sophisticated cyber equipment, along with cybersecurity operatives on board the plane.)

(Our intelligence agencies have been reporting on the growing threat for the last 12+ years. It is not surprising that it started under the Obama administration with a foothold.)

(IRGC) Iran's Revolutionary Guard – Lebanon's Hezbollah, an Iranian proxy, whose activities in Venezuela have further emboldened terrorist activities in the region. Utilizing trade routes to further their financial operations through drug trade and human trafficking, etc.

The growing threat from the Caribbean coast to the United States, as well as through our southern borders, is upon us. It's not a mistake that you're seeing an uptick in so-called Venezuelans coming through the southern border. I reported over a year ago that the Venezuelan government gives proper paperwork to Iranians, saying that they are Venezuelan citizens. Two US-sanctioned airlines fly regular flights back and forth from Venezuela to Tehran.

Our SOUTHCOM Commander Richardson is concerned about the growing threat of China, Iran in this region.

I have a pretty extensive report on the growing threat on our borders (internal and external) called enemies at the gate.

While Republicans and our leaders fight internally, the growing threat continues. There will be terror attacks on our soil. One of my resources let me know that they are conducting mass casualty training events within law enforcement and other agencies. Coupled with hospital systems and strategic cities doing the same for the last year, conducting National Emergency Broadcast Systems, not a coincidence. The writing is on the wall.

IRAN'S GROWING THREAT TO OUR BORDERS-

Iran's influence with Hamas and Hezbollah through financing and delivering weapons is directly responsible for helping to carry out the attacks on Israel. They will continue to remain a threat to Israel, directly through their missile and UAV forces, and indirectly via their support of the Lebanese Hezbollah and other associated forces. Iran's support for Iraqi Shia militias, the Bashar al-Assad regime in Syria, and the Houthis in Yemen through the provision of advanced military systems is a threat to the US and its partners in the region, such as Saudi Arabia. Iran has committed to developing networks inside the U.S. to launch attacks against U.S. forces, soft targets, and persons. Former and current U.S. officials have been threatened in response to the killing of Islamic Revolutionary Guard Corps-Qods Force Commander Qasem Soleimani in January 2020. Previous attempts have been made to conduct lethal assaults inside of the United States without success. (With our open borders, these lethal assault attempts will become a reality).

Iran has continued to grow in strength and influence in Latin America, they use Venezuela as their conduit to enter the region, Iran's Mahan Air operates regular flights between Caracas and Tehran. The United States imposed sanctions on the company in 2011, saying it provided financial and other support to Iran's Islamic Revolutionary Guards (IRGC).

Recently, Iranian President Ebrahim Raisi visited three Latin American countries in mid-June 2023: Venezuela, Nicaragua, and Cuba. With US sanctions on all three, the trip was an opportunity to publish diplomatic statements outlining Iran's convergence with the revolutionary Latin American countries against US pressures and policies. Raisi described the independent, groundbreaking development of the Latin American countries, no longer considered the "backyard of the Americans," paving the way for the search of their own independence. Iran aims to create a collective revolutionary agenda despite the current US-led international order.

After two days of diplomatic visits in Nicaragua, Iran's President Raisi announced the signing of three cooperation memoranda and the creation of a binational joint commission to further develop the agreements between the two countries. The agreements cover a variety of sectors, including judicial affairs, economic exchange, health, pharmaceutical support, and technological and scientific exchange. Venezuelan delegation representatives also signed various cooperation agreements during the event. These are just a few examples of several agreements Iran has made in Latin America.

Iran is further strengthening its influence in Latin America with its support of Venezuelan Hezbollah. Hezbollah has a strong and growing presence in South America, particularly in the Tri-Border Area of Argentina, Brazil, and Paraguay. It is a hub for criminal activities, including drug trafficking, money laundering, and weapons trafficking, among other illicit activities.

Mexico The Threat -

Now that we have highlighted Iran's growing influence in Latin America, let's examine the threat to the U.S. from Mexico. The Biden Administration's wide open border policies are knowingly putting American lives at risk. We know from reports that known terrorists have been flooding our borders. The understaffed, overworked BP agents do not have the capacity to properly vet the thousands invading different sectors of the southern border every day, which spreads across four states and, of course, the downplayed northern border. The media does a good job of covering for the Biden Regime by not reporting on the outrageous number of got-aways, these are those illegally entering the country undetected every day. The Cartel has been operating and growing without impunity or consequence from our own government. In some instances, we are even aiding their movements! This administration's policies have allowed the cartels to gain strength financially and militarily which has aided them to obtain incredibly sophisticated weapons, including the use of UAVs and many other tools in their arsenal.

The Cartels are increasingly relying on drones to map routes and detect vulnerabilities along the US border. Some of the intercepted drones are used for surveillance of Illegal migrants, while others are used to establish the position of the border patrol in order to identify optimal times to transport narcotics or high value assets, weapons and even terrorists over the border!

The growing sophistication in which they are building and using tunnels (explained earlier in article) The Cartels continued support and partnerships with our enemies, like Iran, China, and Russia poses a direct national security threat to the United States, to not secure our borders is an act of treason. (The act of betraying one's country especially by attempting to kill the sovereign).

If we do not gain operational control of our borders and take serious action now, similar to how Iran used Hamas in the Gaza Strip to attack Israel, they will use Hezbollah to attack the U.S. The tunnels created by cartels serve as obvious entry points for bringing in weapons of mass destruction. We must close our borders and secure them now to prevent further unrepairable damage to our national security, unfortunately because of Biden's policies of open borders, I fear America will be the next Israel!

China Threat -

By Photographer: Dati Bendo | Source: Wikipedia

In 2008, the Chinese government issued its first policy paper on Latin America and the Caribbean, putting forward the goal of establishing a comprehensive and cooperative partnership based on equality, mutual benefit, and common development with Latin America and the Caribbean countires. Since then, China's footprint in both Latin America countries, Cuba, the Caribbean, and Canada has strengthened and should be alarming. Through their Belt and Road initiatives, China has gained significant financial influence and control over infrastructure, supply chain routes, agriculture, and more. This has raised serious concerns within our

U.S. Southern Command (SOUTHCOM), which has voiced series concerns to the administration and congress stating that in recent years China's activities in LAC (Latin America Countries) posture asserted that the PRC (People's Republic of China) has "the capability and intent to eschew international norms, advance its brand of authoritarianism, and amass power and influence at the expense of existing and emerging democracies in our hemisphere. "According to SOUTHCOM, the People's Republic of China (PRC) is investing in critical infrastructure, including deep water ports (which can be used for warships), cyber, and space facilities which can have the potential for dual use for malign commercial and military activities

U.S. Southern Command (SOUTHCOM), which has voiced series concerns to the administration and congress stating that in recent years China's activities in LAC (Latin America Countries) posture asserted that the PRC (People's Republic of China) has "the capability and intent to eschew international norms, advance its brand of authoritarianism, and amass power and influence at the expense of existing and emerging democracies in our hemisphere. "According to SOUTHCOM, the People's Republic of China (PRC) is investing in critical infrastructure, including deep water ports (which can be used for warships), cyber, and space facilities which can have the potential for dual use for malign commercial and military activities."

Coupled with their continued presence in Cuba with known spy posts or with our neighbors in Canada through cold weather military drills, open northern borders which expose us to PLA (People's Republic Army) being able to cross into the U.S. undetected, and of course the direct connection with the Mexican drug cartels for which China's role in the production of illicit Fentanyl, a synthetic opioid roughly fifty times more potent than heroin. Currently, most U.S.-destined illicit Fentanyl and Carfentanil comes from Mexico, using chemical precursors sourced from the PRC which kills hundreds of thousand American's each year.

Latin America's Response –

Nicaraguan dictator Daniel Ortega has provided Iran with a platform for its activities in Central America, signing over twenty cooperation agreements and holding meetings with Iranian delegations to strengthen their military cooperation. Despite criticism within Nicaragua, the two countries are forging closer ties in pursuit of a shared agenda.

Venezuela- In 2022, Venezuelan leader Nicolas Maduro signed a 20-year cooperation agreement with Iran that included defense, energy, and gas. In addition, Maduro gave Iran thousands of acres of land for agricultural purposes, cementing his empire-building ambitions. This agreement is sure to have long-term implications for the stability of the region.

Ministers Mohamad Reza Qarai Ashtiani and Edmundo Novillo Aguilar, during the signing of a memorandum of bilateral cooperation between Bolivia and Iran, on July 20, 2023 in Tehran

Cuba receives major support from Iran in the areas of technology, food security, and oil. China also has a major presence through financial ties.

Brazil's President Lula da Silva has recently authorized the entry of Iranian armed destroyers to travel through Latin America. On July 2022, they allowed a U.S.-sanctioned cargo plane to land in Buenos Aires, carrying highly sophisticated cyber intelligence equipment and cyber intelligence operators. The pilot of the plane is from Iran's Revolutionary Guard. This shows that despite international pressure, Iran has successfully gained influence in the Latin American region. Whether these bold and provocative moves signify a shift in the balance of power, only time will tell.

Bolivia has become an increasingly important stronghold for Iran, and recent reports indicate a significant buildup of arms in the region. Iran has established numerous military installations and created a weapons depot in the country in an effort to expand its presence and control in the area. This move is expected to have a long-term impact on the geopolitics of the region.

In response to the Iran-backed Hamas attack on Israel, a strong U.S. ally, the Latin America response from these countries was to show its support for Palestine.

Final Thoughts –

America's leaders are clearly not putting the interests of the United States citizens first. While they send billions upon billions of taxpayer dollars to our enemies like Iran or to Ukraine to protect their borders while our borders remain wide open! The Ukraine cover-up of corruption including our own military allegedly conducting illegal gain-of-function research for military purposes to Burisma illegally placed servers storing data. The weakening of our military, the orchestrated "failed" withdraw of Afghanistan, the wide-open border, the growing strength of the Cartels, the overdosing of our fighting youth and the absence of a government which is by the people and for the people leads us to the only inevitable conclusion - invasion!

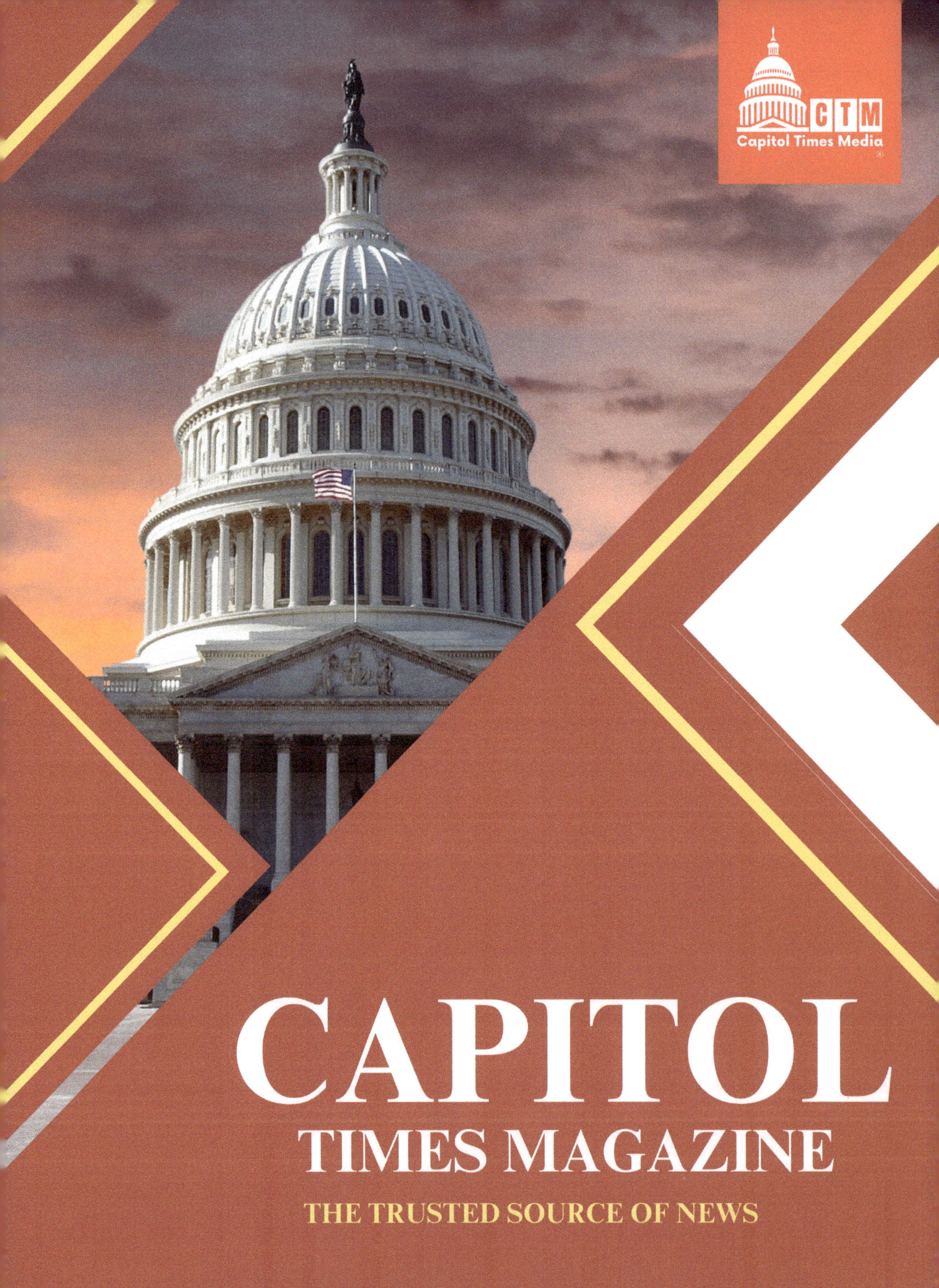
CTM
Capitol Times Media

CAPITOL
TIMES MAGAZINE
THE TRUSTED SOURCE OF NEWS

COLBERT
Business Consulting

We help your business grow faster and better

Contact Us For Consultation

(936) 727-4540

Make America Great Again

MAKE AMERICA
CHRISTIAN AGAIN WITH
TRUMP

A CALL TO FAITH, UNITY, AND TRANSFORMATION IN THE SPIRIT OF TRUMP

BY DANIEL HARRIS

In recent years, America has witnessed significant societal changes, some of which have raised concerns among those who cherish the country's Christian heritage. The call to "Make America Christian Again" is not just a slogan; it represents a deep-seated desire to preserve the values that have been the bedrock of this great nation. In this pursuit, many conservatives find a champion in former President Donald J. Trump, whose policies and principles resonate strongly with the Christian political conservative movement.

PRESERVING RELIGIOUS FREEDOM:

One of the cornerstones of American democracy is the freedom to practice one's faith without fear of persecution. Donald Trump consistently defended religious liberty, ensuring that Christians and people of all faiths could express their beliefs openly and without constraint. His administration worked to protect religious institutions, safeguarding their ability to serve their communities without compromising their beliefs.

DEFENDING THE SANCTITY OF LIFE:

Central to the Christian and conservative worldview is the sanctity of human life. Donald Trump stood firmly in the pro-life camp, advocating for policies that protected the unborn. By appointing judges who respect the Constitution and its original intent, Trump helped pave the way for a potential reevaluation of laws that have enabled abortion on demand.

CHAMPIONING TRADITIONAL FAMILY VALUES:

The family unit, as defined by traditional Christian values, has been the cornerstone of civilizations for millennia. Former President Trump's administration upheld these values, supporting policies that strengthened families and encouraged stability. By promoting marriage, parental rights, and educational freedom, his policies aimed to create an environment where families could thrive, passing down essential moral and ethical principles to the next generation. We hope he will keep his policies more Christian when he wins the White House in 2024.

CHAMPIONING TRADITIONAL FAMILY VALUES:

The family unit, as defined by traditional Christian values, has been the cornerstone of civilizations for millennia. President Trump's administration upheld these values, supporting policies that strengthened families and encouraged stability. By promoting marriage, parental rights, and educational freedom, his policies aimed to create an environment where families could thrive, passing down essential moral and ethical principles to the next generation.

UPHOLDING CONSERVATIVE PRINCIPLES:

Christian conservatives often find common ground with Trump's stance on limited government, individual responsibility, and free-market capitalism. Donald Trump economic policies spurred job growth, reduced unemployment, and created opportunities for all Americans, fostering an environment where citizens could provide for their families and contribute meaningfully to society.

PROTECTING NATIONAL SECURITY:

In an ever-changing world, safeguarding the nation is paramount. Trump's commitment to a robust national defense and secure borders resonated with many conservative Christians. By addressing immigration concerns and ensuring a strong military, he aimed to protect American citizens, their families, and their way of life.

In the pursuit to "Make America Christian Again," it is crucial to recognize that this vision is not about exclusion but about preserving the principles that have made America a beacon of hope and freedom for people worldwide. While no leader is perfect, many conservative Christians believe that Donald Trump's policies and dedication to these core values align with their vision for a strong and prosperous nation.

As America moves forward, the call to uphold Christian values should serve as a unifying force, guiding the nation toward a future where faith, freedom, and family are cherished, protected, and celebrated. With thoughtful consideration and respectful dialogue, it is possible to work together, regardless of political affiliations, to ensure that America remains a land where Christian principles are not just remembered but actively practiced, making the nation stronger and more compassionate for all its citizens.

THE DARK REALITY OF PALESTINIAN POLITICAL CULTURE:

A Conservative Perspective

By Jonathan Abijah

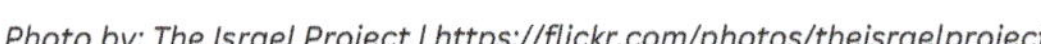
Photo by: The Israel Project | https://flickr.com/photos/theisraelproject

In the sun-soaked lands of southern Israel, where olive trees sway gently in the breeze and ancient history whispers through the winds, a tragedy unfolded. A day of unspeakable horror, where waves of evil engulfed the region. The merciless onslaught of anti-Zionism and anti-Semitism converged, creating a macabre dance of hatred. Elders were slaughtered, toddlers kidnapped, and innocent souls mowed down. Synagogue-goers' corpses lay desecrated, and the survivors were left to carry the burden of emotional and physical scars until their last breaths.

This dark day serves as a stark reminder of the fatal flaw embedded within Palestinian political culture – a sadism that seeks solace in bloodshed. As the world watched in horror, the events of October 7 underscored the depth of this issue. To some, this day might be seen as a victory, a triumph over the perceived oppressor. But what does it truly say about a people when their greatest achievement is measured in blood and despair?

In the face of such brutality, Israel finds itself compelled to defend its very existence vigorously. The proximity of hills, just an RPG shot away from Ben-Gurion Airport's runways, reminds us of the constant threat that looms. The world witnesses why trusting those who revel in violence becomes an insurmountable challenge.

The rampage through southern Israel was not just an isolated incident; it revealed the core of the Palestinian victory plan. It validated Golda Meir's timeless statement: "If the Arabs put down their weapons today, there would be no more violence. If the Jews put down their weapons today, there would be no more Israel." These words resonate with chilling accuracy even today, emphasizing the essential need for self-defense in the face of unrelenting hatred.

Beyond the borders of the conflict zone, Palestinians export this venomous hatred abroad. Their focus, it seems, is not on nation-building but on tearing down others. This obsession manifests in events like Israel Apartheid Week on campuses worldwide, where energies are dedicated to denigrating Israel instead of fostering their own progress.

History tells us that no nationalist movement can thrive if its identity revolves solely around negating others. Such an approach only fuels the flames of hatred, breeding dictatorship rather than democracy and perpetual wars instead of peaceful coexistence. The internal politics of Palestine, marred by factionalism and violence, reflects the deep-seated nihilism that hampers progress.

However, it is crucial to recognize that this critique is not a blanket statement applied to every individual Palestinian. It acknowledges a historical phenomenon and a cultural trend deeply embedded within certain circles. Despite this grim reality, it is not an assertion that peace with Palestinians is unattainable. Many Arabs, adapting to the changing tides of history and Israeli power, have found ways to coexist peacefully.

In conclusion, the events of October 7 and the subsequent reactions worldwide remind us of the complexities that surround the Israeli-Palestinian conflict. It is imperative to confront the deep-seated cultural issues that perpetuate violence and hatred. Only through understanding, dialogue, and a collective commitment to peace can a resolution be found. In the face of darkness, the glimmer of hope lies in the hearts of those who strive for genuine peace, transcending the boundaries of religion, ethnicity, and politics.

Photo By: The Israel Project | https://flickr.com/photos/theisraelproject

WHO IS STEVE SCALISE?

By Mary Gill

In the midst of the political whirlwind surrounding the race to elect a new Speaker of the House, one name has emerged as a prominent contender: Representative Steve Scalise. As the nation eagerly watches this high-stakes battle unfold, it's essential to understand the background and potential leadership of the man in the spotlight.

Who is Rep. Steve Scalise?

Representative Steve Scalise, a seasoned politician from Louisiana, has been a prominent figure in American politics for years. Born on October 6, 1965, in New Orleans, Scalise graduated from Louisiana State University with a degree in computer programming. His political journey began in the Louisiana state legislature, where he served from 1996 to 2008. In 2008, he was elected to the United States House of Representatives, where he has represented Louisiana's 1st congressional district since.

In the bustling corridors of Capitol Hill, where the political fervor often overshadows personal beliefs, stands a man whose faith serves as a guiding light, illuminating his path through the complexities of American governance. Representative Steve Scalise, a devout Christian, has become a testament to the enduring power of faith in the realm of politics.

A Foundation of Faith

Born on October 6, 1965, in New Orleans, Louisiana, Steve Scalise's faith journey began at an early age. Raised in a devout Catholic family, he imbibed the values of compassion, kindness, and service. These foundational principles would later shape his political career, anchoring him amidst the stormy seas of politics.

Scalise's Christian faith isn't just a Sunday ritual; it's a driving force behind his decisions and actions. He often speaks about how his beliefs inspire him to serve his constituents with dedication and integrity, values he believes are deeply rooted in his religious convictions.

Faith in Action

One of the most compelling aspects of Rep. Scalise's faith is its embodiment in his actions. In 2002, he was elected to the U.S. House of Representatives, representing Louisiana's 1st congressional district. Throughout his tenure, he consistently advocated for policies that align with his Christian beliefs, including pro-life stances and support for traditional family values.

Even in the face of adversity, Scalise's faith remained unshaken. In 2017, he survived a horrific shooting during a congressional baseball practice, an incident that tested his resilience and faith. His recovery was nothing short of a miracle, a testament to his unwavering trust in a higher power.

Scalise's Christian faith has not only been a personal guiding light but also a bridge-builder in the often divisive world of politics. Regardless of party lines, his colleagues recognize his genuine commitment to his beliefs, which fosters respect and understanding among peers with diverse backgrounds and perspectives.

His willingness to engage in meaningful conversations about faith has encouraged dialogue and unity, reminding everyone that spirituality can be a unifying force rather than a divisive one.

In an era where political polarization often dominates the headlines, Rep. Steve Scalise stands out as a beacon of hope, reminding the nation that faith and politics can coexist harmoniously. His story serves as an inspiration to aspiring politicians, encouraging them to integrate their beliefs into their public service, fostering a more compassionate and understanding political landscape.

As Rep. Steve Scalise continues his journey in the hallowed halls of Congress, his Christian faith remains a steadfast foundation upon which he builds his legacy. His story challenges us all to reflect on the role of faith in our lives, urging us to consider how we can infuse our beliefs into our actions, creating a more empathetic and just society for everyone.

POLITICAL CAREER AND ACCOMPLISHMENTS

DURING HIS TIME IN THE HOUSE, SCALISE HAS MADE A SIGNIFICANT IMPACT ON VARIOUS POLICY ISSUES. HE HAS BEEN A STAUNCH ADVOCATE FOR CONSERVATIVE PRINCIPLES, FOCUSING ON ECONOMIC GROWTH, HEALTHCARE REFORM, AND NATIONAL SECURITY. SCALISE HAS ALSO PLAYED A PIVOTAL ROLE IN THE REPUBLICAN PARTY, SERVING AS THE HOUSE MAJORITY WHIP FROM 2014 TO 2019, WHERE HE WAS RESPONSIBLE FOR RALLYING PARTY MEMBERS AND ENSURING VOTES ON KEY LEGISLATION.

Leadership Qualities

Scalise's leadership qualities have shone brightly, particularly during challenging times. One of the most notable instances was in 2017 when he survived a targeted shooting during a congressional baseball practice. His resilience and determination in the face of adversity garnered widespread respect from both sides of the aisle, showcasing his ability to lead under pressure.

Challenges and Opportunities Ahead

If elected as the Speaker of the House, Scalise would face a myriad of challenges, including addressing the ongoing Russia-Ukraine and Hamas-Israel wars, economic recovery, climate change, and social justice issues. His approach to these challenges and ability to build bipartisan relationships will play a crucial role in shaping the legislative agenda and the direction of the country.

Conclusion

All eyes are on Representative Steve Scalise. With a wealth of political experience, a proven track record, and resilience in the face of adversity, Scalise stands as a strong contender for this influential position and Pro-Trump Politician. The nation waits in anticipation to see how this seasoned politician will navigate the complex political landscape and potentially shape the future of the United States House of Representatives.

STAY TUNED TO OUR

Freedom

FOURUM

SHOW

EVERY THURSDAY - FRIDAY

8:00 PM - WWW.CAPITOLTIMESMEDIA.COM

FACEBOOK @CAPITOLTIMES | CTM NEWS

Hosted by

DAVID
COLBERT

REQUEST LINE:
972-591-8859

LIVE STREAM AT:
WWW.CAPITOLTIMESMEDIA.COM
FACEBOOK: @CAPITOLTIMES - [CTM NEWS]

BIDEN'S VISION FOR 'CLIMATE CORPS' SPARKS CONTROVERSY IN ENVIRONMENTAL CIRCLES

BY Mary Gill

In the face of global climate challenges, the Biden administration's recent launch of the American Climate Corps has sparked a national conversation about the most effective path to environmental progress. While the program's objectives are commendable, critics argue that growing government and burdening future generations with more debt is not the solution. Instead, they advocate for a more pragmatic approach that empowers the private sector and individuals, removes government barriers to conservation, and saves taxpayers money.

President Biden's Climate Corps initiative, aimed at recruiting young Americans to engage in conservation efforts, comes at a time of low unemployment and record-high federal spending. With the U.S. national debt soaring to $33 trillion, concerns about fiscal responsibility have taken center stage. Critics argue that redundant government programs, financed through increased appropriations and future taxes, are not the answer. Rather, they contend that existing private sector initiatives and federal programs such as the Foundation for Food and Agriculture Research (FFAR), Environmental Quality Incentives Program (EQIP), and Conservation Stewardship Program (CSP) are proving to be effective models.

The FFAR, a non-profit organization, leverages both public and private funding to support innovative research in areas critical to sustainable agriculture such as soil health, next-generation crops, and water management. The beauty of this program lies in its ability to match every dollar of federal funding with private-sector contributions, magnifying the impact of the federal investment and encouraging private participation.

Similarly, the EQIP and CSP initiatives have successfully removed obstacles for farmers and landowners engaged in conservation work. By empowering local landowners to devise tailored solutions to their unique challenges, these programs encourage bottom-up innovation and problem-solving. Critics of the Climate Corps argue that redirecting funds from wasteful government programs to support these existing initiatives is a more responsible use of taxpayers' money.

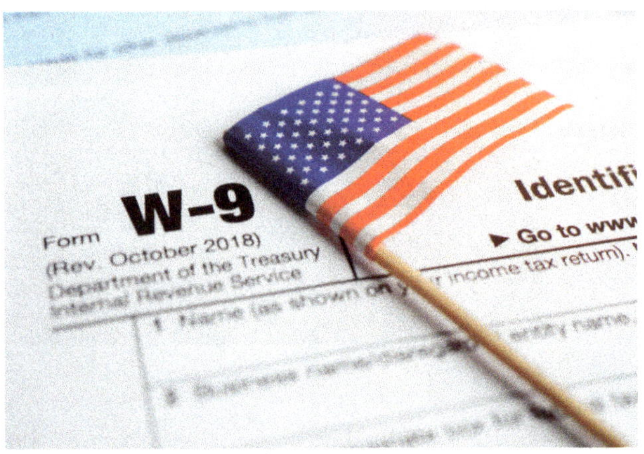

The prevailing sentiment among critics is that a pragmatic approach, which enables private sector innovation and removes bureaucratic hurdles, is key to tackling the environmental challenges we face. They argue that the government should focus on creating an environment conducive to private sector involvement rather than creating new, potentially redundant, programs. By doing so, the nation can achieve meaningful climate progress without burdening future generations with staggering debts.

In essence, the conversation surrounding environmental progress should shift from merely allocating funds to empowering the private sector, fostering innovation, and encouraging individual initiatives. By embracing this approach, the nation can pave the way for a sustainable future without compromising its economic stability or burdening its youth with the weight of excessive debt.

CONCLUSION

The path to environmental progress is not paved solely with good intentions but requires a pragmatic and responsible approach. While the American Climate Corps embodies noble aspirations, it is imperative to question the necessity of additional government programs when viable alternatives already exist. By empowering the private sector, encouraging innovation, and redirecting funds from wasteful endeavors to impactful initiatives, the United States can chart a course towards environmental sustainability without compromising its economic stability. It is only through such concerted efforts that the nation can strike a balance between conservation, economic growth, and fiscal responsibility, ensuring a brighter future for generations to come.

STAY TUNED TO OUR
Freedom
FOURUM
SHOW
EVERY THURSDAY - FRIDAY
8:00 PM - WWW.CAPITOLTIMESMEDIA.COM
FACEBOOK @CAPITOLTIMES | CTM NEWS
DAVID COLBERT
Hosted by
REQUEST LINE:
972-591-8859
LIVE STREAM AT:
WWW.CAPITOLTIMESMEDIA.COM
FACEBOOK: @CAPITOLTIMES - [CTM NEWS]

STAND WITH ISRAEL

SHOW YOUR SUPPORT FOR ISRAEL AND ITS PEOPLE

We believe that Israel has the right to defend itself against terrorism and threats to its security. Join us in supporting Israel's right to exist and thrive as a nation. Together for Israel

LET'S UNITE IN SOLIDARITY WITH ISRAEL AND ITS PEOPLE.

Let's extend our support, empathy, and prayers to the people of Israel, advocating for peace, understanding, and harmony in the region. Together, we can bridge divides and nurture a world where every individual, regardless of nationality or religion, can live in peace and security.

Stay Informed with Capitol Times Magazine!

**Your Ultimate Source for US National News, Right in the Heart of Capitol.
Grab Your Copy Today and Stay Ahead of the Times!**

https://capitoltimesmedia.com

Iran's Alleged Involvement in Devastating Israel Attack Raises Global Concerns

By James Hall

> **"Iran's President Ebrahim Raisi said on Sunday 8th October 2023 that Tehran supports the Palestinians' right to self-defense and warned Israel must be held accountable for endangering the region, a day after Hamas attacked Israel."**

On October 7, 2023, a devastating Hamas terrorist attack on Israel, leaving the WORLD in shock and mourning. Investigations are underway to determine the full extent of the assault, with mounting evidence pointing toward Iran's involvement. If proven true, this attack poses a significant threat to regional security and stability.

Evidence of Iran's Involvement

Experts have been meticulously analyzing the available evidence, revealing compelling indications of Iran's hand in the attack:

President of Iran | Photo Source: Wikipedia

1. Weaponry: The weapons used in the assault bear similarities to those previously linked to Iran, including sophisticated drone technology and precision-guided missiles, showcasing Iran's advanced military capabilities.

2. Proxy Attacks: Iran has a well-documented history of employing proxy groups to orchestrate attacks in the region, mirroring the modus operandi seen in this incident, consistent with previous attacks attributed to Iran.

3. Motives: Iran has openly expressed hostile intentions toward Israel, making the attack a possible component of their broader agenda to destabilize the region and undermine Israel's security.

4. Intelligence Reports: Numerous intelligence reports from various nations have raised concerns about Iran's support for militant groups and their involvement in regional conflicts, further implicating Iran in the attack.

5. Expanding Influence: Iran has been actively expanding its influence in the Middle East. This attack could be interpreted as a strategic move to assert dominance and intimidate regional adversaries.

Implications for Regional Security

The alleged Iranian involvement in the attack carries grave implications for regional security:

1. Escalation of Tensions: The incident could lead to heightened tensions between Iran and Israel, potentially sparking a dangerous cycle of retaliation and counterattacks, exacerbating an already volatile situation.

2. Destabilization: The Middle East is grappling with conflicts and instability. Iran's involvement in attacks further exacerbates the region's fragility, potentially escalating existing conflicts.

3. Global Impact: Beyond the region, the attack raises concerns for international security, increasing the potential for further terrorist activities worldwide, demanding enhanced global cooperation in counterterrorism efforts.

4. Deteriorating Diplomatic Relations: If Iran's involvement is substantiated, it would strain diplomatic relations between Iran and other nations, leading to increased isolation and strained international cooperation.

Conclusion

While investigations into the attack in Israel are ongoing, the mounting evidence strongly suggests Iran's involvement. This situation underscores the urgent need for swift and decisive measures to address Iran's aggressive actions. The international community must collaborate to counter such threats effectively, safeguard regional security, and preserve global stability. The implications of these findings reach far beyond the borders of the Middle East, emphasizing the critical importance of diplomatic resolutions and international cooperation in maintaining peace and security worldwide.

HAMAS VS ISRAEL: ARMORY EXPLAINED –

An American Perspective

By David K.Wood

The ongoing conflict between Israel and Hamas is a complex and deeply rooted issue with historical, political, and humanitarian dimensions. In this article, we will focus on the military aspects of the conflict, examining the armories of both parties involved and US-Israel relations. It is important to note that this analysis is presented from a pro-Israel perspective, aiming to provide an objective overview of the military capabilities and strategies employed by Israel and Hamas.

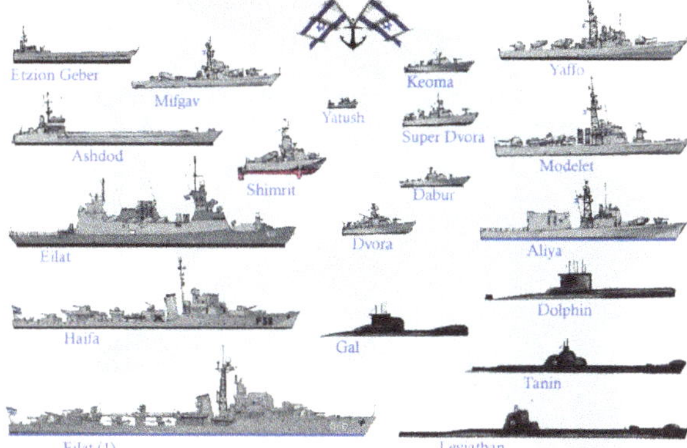

Israel's Advanced Military Technology:

Israel boasts one of the most advanced and sophisticated military forces in the world. Its arsenal includes state-of-the-art aircraft, tanks, naval vessels, missile defense systems, and intelligence capabilities. The Israel Defense Forces (IDF) invest heavily in research and development, ensuring their military technology remains cutting-edge.

1. Air Force:

The Israeli Air Force (IAF) operates advanced fighter jets such as the F-15 and F-16, capable of precision airstrikes. Israel also possesses unmanned aerial vehicles (UAVs) like the Heron and Hermes, providing real-time intelligence and surveillance capabilities.

2. Ground Forces:

Israel's ground forces are equipped with modern main battle tanks like the Merkava series, known for their advanced armor and firepower. Additionally, the IDF employs infantry fighting vehicles and artillery systems, ensuring a robust ground presence.

2. Ground Forces:

Israel's ground forces are equipped with modern main battle tanks like the Merkava series, known for their advanced armor and firepower. Additionally, the IDF employs infantry fighting vehicles and artillery systems, ensuring a robust ground presence.

3. Naval Power:

Israel maintains a formidable naval fleet, including advanced corvettes and missile boats armed with cutting-edge anti-ship missiles. This naval force acts as a vital component of Israel's defense strategy, safeguarding its coastline and maritime interests.

4. Missile Defense:

Israel's missile defense system, Iron Dome, intercepts and destroys incoming rockets, providing a critical layer of protection against Hamas' rocket attacks. This technology has saved countless lives by neutralizing threats before they reach populated areas.

Why Israel US Trusted Ally

The United States and Israel have shared a unique and robust alliance since Israel's establishment in 1948. This bond is evident in the substantial military aid provided by the United States to Israel over the years. The aid package, often a topic of intense debate, is a testament to the strong bilateral relations between the two nations. In this article, we will explore the reasons behind the US military aid to Israel and the perspectives of those who support this alliance.

Historical Context

The origins of the strong US-Israel relationship can be traced back to shared democratic values and strategic interests. The United States views Israel as a stable democracy in a region often marked by political volatility. Additionally, Israel's military superiority is seen as a stabilizing force, contributing to the overall security of the Middle East.

BIBLICAL CONNECTIONS

For American Christians, the bond between the United States and Israel is deeply rooted in religious beliefs. The Bible, the holy scripture for Christians, contains numerous references to the land of Israel and its significance in the context of faith. Christians believe that supporting Israel is a way to fulfill biblical prophecies and promises. This perspective often translates into political support, including military aid, as a means to protect and preserve the nation of Israel.

Shared Democratic Values

Both the United States and Israel share a commitment to democratic principles, rule of law, and individual freedoms. In a region where these values are not always prevalent, Israel stands out as a democratic oasis. Christians view Israel as a beacon of democracy in the Middle East and see U.S. military aid as a way to reinforce these shared values and promote stability in the region.

The history of Jewish persecution, culminating in the Holocaust, has evoked strong empathy among Christians. The establishment of Israel as a homeland for the Jewish people after World War II is viewed by Christians as a just and necessary response to centuries of anti-Semitic atrocities. Consequently, supporting Israel, including providing military aid, is seen as a moral imperative, ensuring the safety and security of the Jewish people.

Geopolitical Considerations

From a geopolitical standpoint, Israel is considered a strategic ally for the United States in the Middle East. It provides valuable intelligence, military cooperation, and a stabilizing influence in a region often marred by conflicts and tensions. U.S. military aid to Israel is perceived as an investment in regional security, deterring potential threats and promoting stability in the broader Middle East.

Economic and Technological Collaboration

Beyond military aid, the relationship between the U.S. and Israel extends to economic and technological collaboration. Israel is renowned for its innovation and technological advancements, particularly in areas like cybersecurity, healthcare, and agriculture. This collaboration not only benefits both nations economically but also fosters a sense of partnership and mutual respect, strengthening the ties between the two countries.

Hamas' Weaponry:

In contrast to Israel's advanced military capabilities, Hamas relies on a diverse range of weapons, often procured from various sources. Hamas' arsenal includes rudimentary rockets, mortars, and small arms, which lack the precision and technological sophistication of Israel's weaponry.

1. Rockets and Mortars:

Hamas primarily employs short-range rockets and mortars, with limited accuracy and payload capacity. These weapons pose a significant threat to civilian populations, but their indiscriminate nature contrasts sharply with Israel's precision-guided munitions.

2. Tunnels:

Hamas has constructed a network of tunnels used for various purposes, including smuggling and military operations. While these tunnels have been a concern for Israel, the IDF has developed advanced tunnel-detection technologies to neutralize this threat effectively.

Conclusion:

The conflict between Israel and Hamas is undeniably complex, with deeply rooted historical, political, and social factors. From a military perspective, Israel's advanced weaponry and technology provide it with a significant advantage in terms of precision, effectiveness, and protection of civilian lives. While Hamas continues to pose a threat with its rocket attacks and tunnel systems, Israel's commitment to defense and innovation ensures the safety and security of its citizens remain top priorities.

#ISTANDWITHISRAEL
UNITED WE STAND, DIVIDED WE FALL.
SUPPORT ISRAEL'S RIGHT TO DEFEND ITSELF.

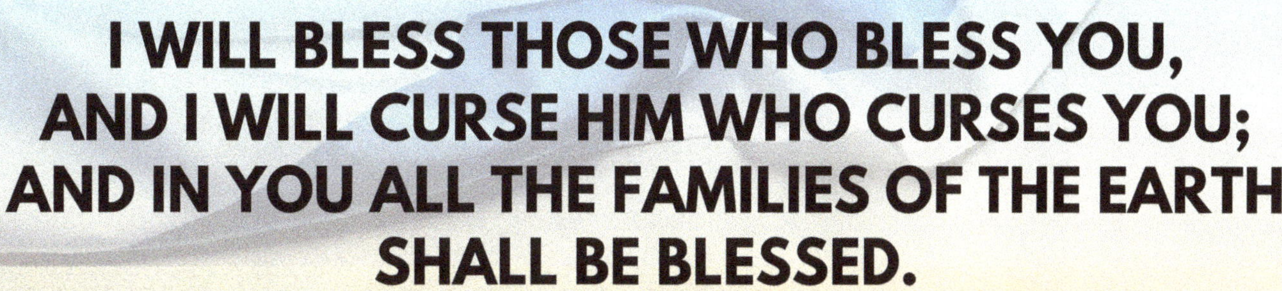

I WILL BLESS THOSE WHO BLESS YOU,
AND I WILL CURSE HIM WHO CURSES YOU;
AND IN YOU ALL THE FAMILIES OF THE EARTH
SHALL BE BLESSED.

Genesis 12:3

Stay Informed with Capitol Times Magazine!

Your Ultimate Source for US National News, Right in the Heart of Capitol.
Grab Your Copy Today and Stay Ahead of the Times!

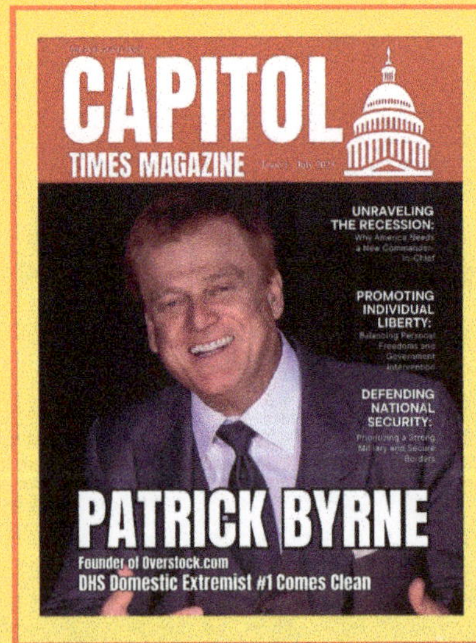

https://capitoltimesmedia.com